Lean and Green Diet Recipes

Quick, Easy and Delicious Recipes to Boost Brain Health and Reverse Disease

Gina Williams

TABLE OF CONTENTS

BREAKFAST RECIPES

1. Millet Porridge

Preparation Time: 10 minutes

Cooking Time: 20 minutes

Servings: 2

Ingredients:

- Sea salt

- 1 tbsp. finely chopped coconuts

- 1/2 cup unsweetened coconut milk
- 1/2 cup rinsed and drained millet
- 1-1/2 cups alkaline water
- 3 drops liquid stevia

Directions:

1. Sauté the millet in a non-stick skillet for about 3 minutes.
2. Add salt and water then stir.
3. Let the meal boil then reduce the amount of heat.
4. Cook for 15 minutes then add the remaining ingredients. Stir.
5. Cook the meal for 4 extra minutes.
6. Serve the meal with toping of the chopped nuts.

Nutrition: Calories: 219 kcal Fat: 4.5g Carbs: 38.2g Protein: 6.4g

2. Jackfruit Vegetable Fry

Preparation Time: 5 minutes

Cooking Time: 5 minutes

Servings: 6

Ingredients:

- 2 finely chopped small onions
- 2 cups finely chopped cherry tomatoes
- 1/8 tsp. ground turmeric
- 1 tbsp. olive oil
- 2 seeded and chopped red bell peppers
- 3 cups seeded and chopped firm jackfruit
- 1/8 tsp. cayenne pepper
- 2 tbsps. chopped fresh basil leaves
- Salt

Directions:

1. In a greased skillet, sauté the onions and bell peppers for about 5 minutes.
2. Add the tomatoes then stir.
3. Cook for 2 minutes.
4. Then add the jackfruit, cayenne pepper, salt, and turmeric.

5. Cook for about 8 minutes.

6. Garnish the meal with basil leaves.

7. Serve warm.

Nutrition: Calories: 236 kcal Fat: 1.8g Carbs: 48.3g Protein: 7g

3. Fried egg with bacon

Preparation Time: 5 minutes

Cooking Time: 10 minutes

Servings: 1

Ingredients:

- 2 eggs
- 30 grams of bacon
- 2 tbsp olive oil
- salt
- pepper

Directions:

1. Heat oil in the pan and fry the bacon.
2. Reduce the heat and beat the eggs in the pan.
3. Cook the eggs and season with salt and pepper.
4. Serve the fried eggs hot with the bacon.

Nutrition: kcal: 405 Carbohydrates: 1 g Protein: 19 g Fat: 38 g

4. Smoothie bowl with berries, poppy seeds, nuts and seeds

Preparation Time: 15 minutes

Cooking Time: 0 minutes

Servings: 2

Ingredients:

- 5 chopped almonds
- 2 chopped walnuts
- 1 apple
- ¼ banana
- 300 g yogurt
- 60 g raspberries
- 20 g blueberries
- 20 g rolled oats, roasted in a pan
- 10 g poppy seeds
- 1 teaspoon pumpkin seeds
- Agave syrup

Directions:

1. Clean the fruit and let it drain.
2. Take some berries and set them aside.
3. Place the remaining berries in a tall mixing vessel.

4. Cut the banana into slices. Put a few aside.

5. Add the rest of the banana to the berries.

6. Remove the core of the apple and cut it into quarters.

7. Cut the quarters into thin wedges and set a few aside.

8. Add the remaining wedges to the berries.

9. Add the yogurt to the fruits and mix everything into a puree.

10. Sweeten the smoothie with the agave syrup.

11. Divide it into two bowls.

12. Serve it with the remaining fruit, poppy seeds, oatmeal, nuts and seeds.

Nutrition: kcal: 284 Carbohydrates: 21 g Protein: 11 g Fat: 19 g

5. Whole grain bread and avocado

Preparation Time: 5 minutes

Cooking Time: 0 minutes

Serving: 1

Ingredients:

- 2 slices of wholemeal bread
- 60 g of cottage cheese
- 1 stick of thyme
- ½ avocado
- ½ lime
- Chili flakes
- salt
- pepper

Directions:

1. Cut the avocado in half.
2. Remove the pulp and cut it into slices.
3. Pour the lime juice over it.
4. Wash the thyme and shake it dry.
5. Remove the leaves from the stem.
6. Brush the whole wheat bread with the cottage cheese.
7. Place the avocado slices on top.

8. Top with the chili flakes and thyme.

9. Add salt and pepper and serve.

Nutrition: kcal: 490 Carbohydrates: 31 g Protein: 19 g Fat: 21 g

6. Porridge with walnuts

Preparation Time: 5 minutes

Cooking Time: 10 minutes

Servings: 1

Ingredients:

- 50 g raspberries
- 50 g blueberries
- 25 g of ground walnuts
- 20 g of crushed flaxseed
- 10 g of oatmeal
- 200 ml nut drink
- Agave syrup
- ½ teaspoon cinnamon
- salt

Directions:

1. Warm the nut drink in a small saucepan.
2. Add the walnuts, flaxseed, and oatmeal, stirring constantly.
3. Stir in the cinnamon and salt.
4. Simmer for 8 minutes.
5. Keep stirring everything.

6. Sweet the whole thing.

7. Put the porridge in a bowl.

8. Wash the berries and let them drain.

9. Add them to the porridge and serve everything.

Nutrition: kcal: 378 Carbohydrates: 11 g Protein: 18 g Fat: 27 g

7. Alkaline Blueberry Spelt Pancakes

Preparation Time: 6 minutes

Cooking Time: 20 minutes

Servings: 3

Ingredients:

- 2 cups Spelt Flour
- 1 cup Coconut Milk
- 1/2 cup Alkaline Water
- 2 tbsps. Grapeseed Oil
- 1/2 cup Agave
- 1/2 cup Blueberries
- 1/4 tsp. Sea Moss

Directions:

1. Mix the spelt flour, agave, grapeseed oil, hemp seeds, and the sea moss together in a bowl.
2. Add in 1 cup of hemp milk and alkaline water to the mixture, until you get the consistency mixture you like.
3. Crimp the blueberries into the batter.
4. Heat the skillet to moderate heat then lightly coat it with the grapeseed oil.

5. Pour the batter into the skillet then let them cook for approximately 5 minutes on every side.

6. Serve and Enjoy.

Nutrition: Calories: 203 kcal Fat: 1.4g Carbs: 41.6g Proteins: 4.8g

8. Alkaline Blueberry Muffins

Preparation Time: 5 Minutes

Cooking Time: 20 minutes

Servings: 3

Ingredients:

- 1 cup Coconut Milk
- 3/4 cup Spelt Flour
- 3/4 Teff Flour
- 1/2 cup Blueberries
- 1/3 cup Agave
- 1/4 cup Sea Moss Gel
- 1/2 tsp. Sea Salt
- Grapeseed Oil

Directions:

1. Adjust the temperature of the oven to 365 degrees.
2. Grease 6 regular-size muffin cups with muffin liners.
3. In a bowl, mix together sea salt, sea moss, agave, coconut milk, and flour gel until they are properly blended.
4. You then crimp in blueberries.
5. Coat the muffin pan lightly with the grapeseed oil.

6. Pour in the muffin batter.

7. Bake for at least 30 minutes until it turns golden brown.

8. Serve.

Nutrition: Calories: 160 kcal Fat: 5gCarbs: 25g Proteins: 2g

LUNCH

9. Chicken Omelet

Preparation Time: 5 minutes

Cooking Time: 15 minutes

Servings: 1

Ingredients:

- 2 bacon slices; cooked and crumbled
- 2 eggs
- 1 tablespoon homemade mayonnaise
- 1 tomato; chopped.
- 1-ounce rotisserie chicken; shredded
- 1 teaspoon mustard
- 1 small avocado; pitted, peeled and chopped.
- Salt and black pepper to the taste.

Directions:

1. In a bowl, mix eggs with some salt and pepper and whisk gently.

2. Heat up a pan over medium heat; spray with some cooking oil, add eggs and cook your omelet for 5 minutes

3. Add chicken, avocado, tomato, bacon, mayo and mustard on one half of the omelet.

4. Fold omelet, cover pan and cook for 5 minutes more

5. Transfer to a plate and serve

Nutrition: Calories: 400 Fat: 32 Fiber: 6 Carbs: 4 Protein: 25

10. Special Almond Cereal

Preparation Time: 5 minutes

Cooking Time: 5 minutes

Servings: 1

Ingredients:

- 2 tablespoons almonds; chopped.
- 1/3 cup coconut milk
- 1 tablespoon chia seeds
- 2 tablespoon pepitas; roasted
- A handful blueberries
- 1 small banana; chopped.
- 1/3 cup water

Directions:

1. In a bowl, mix chia seeds with coconut milk and leave aside for 5 minutes

2. In your food processor, mix half of the pepitas with almonds and pulse them well.

3. Add this to chia seeds mix.

4. Also add the water and stir.

5. Top with the rest of the pepitas, banana pieces and blueberries and serve

Nutrition: Calories: 200 Fat: 3 Fiber: 2 Carbs: 5 Protein: 4

11. Awesome Avocado Muffins

Preparation Time: 10 minutes

Cooking Time: 20 minutes

Servings: 12

Ingredients:

- 6 bacon slices; chopped.
- 1 yellow onion; chopped.
- 1/2 teaspoon baking soda
- 1/2 cup coconut flour
- 1 cup coconut milk
- 2 cups avocado; pitted, peeled and chopped.
- 4 eggs
- Salt and black pepper to the taste.

Directions:

1. Heat up a pan, add onion and bacon; stir and brown for a few minutes
2. In a bowl, mash avocado pieces with a fork and whisk well with the eggs
3. Add milk, salt, pepper, baking soda and coconut flour and stir everything.
4. Add bacon mix and stir again.

5. Add coconut oil to muffin tray, divide eggs and avocado mix into the tray, heat oven at 350 degrees F and bake for 20 minutes

6. Divide muffins between plates and serve them for breakfast.

Nutrition: Calories: 200 Fat: 7 Fiber: 4 Carbs: 7 Protein: 5

12. Tasty WW Pancakes

Preparation Time: 12 minutes

Cooking Time: 3 minutes

Servings: 4

Ingredients:

- 2 ounces' cream cheese
- 1 teaspoon stevia
- 1/2 teaspoon cinnamon; ground
- 2 eggs
- Cooking spray

Directions:

1. Mix the eggs with the cream cheese, stevia, and cinnamon In a blender, and mix well.
2. Heat pan with cooking spray over medium high heat. add 1/4 of the batter, spread well, cook 2 minutes, invert and cook 1 minute more
3. Move to a plate and repeat with the rest of the dough.
4. Serve them right away.

Nutrition: Calories: 344 Fat: 23 Fiber: 12 Carbs: 3 Protein: 16

DINNER

13. Mu Shu Lunch Pork

Preparation Time: 5 minutes

Cooking Time: 10 minutes

Servings: 2

Ingredients:

- 4 cups coleslaw mix, with carrots
- 1 small onion, sliced thin
- 1 lb. cooked roast pork, cut into ½" cubes
- 2 tbsp. hoisin sauce
- 2 tbsp. soy sauce

Directions:

1. In a large skillet, heat the oil on a high heat.
2. Stir-fry the cabbage and onion for 4 minutes until tender.
3. Add the pork, hoisin and soy sauce.
4. Cook until browned.
5. Enjoy!

Nutrition: Calories: 388 Carbs: 16 g Fat: 21 g Protein: 25 g Fiber: 16 g

14. Fiery Jalapeno Poppers

Preparation Time: 10 minutes

Cooking Time: 40 minutes

Servings: 4

Ingredients:

- 5 oz. cream cheese
- ¼ cup mozzarella cheese
- 8 medium jalapeno peppers
- ½ tsp Mrs. Dash Table Blend
- 8 slices bacon

Directions:

1. Preheat your fryer to 400°F/200°C.
2. Cut the jalapenos in half.
3. Use a spoon to scrape out the insides of the peppers.
4. In a bowl, add together the cream cheese, mozzarella cheese and spices of your choice.
5. Pack the cream cheese mixture into the jalapenos and place the peppers on top.
6. Wrap each pepper in 1 slice of bacon, starting from the bottom and working up.
7. Bake for 30 minutes. Broil for an additional 3 minutes.

8. Serve!

Nutrition: Calories: 238 Carbs: 4 g Fat: 10 g Protein: 24 g Fiber: 14 g

15. Bacon & Chicken Patties

Preparation Time: 5 minutes

Cooking Time: 15 minutes

Servings: 2

Ingredients:

- 1 ½ oz. can chicken breast
- 4 slices bacon
- ¼ cup parmesan cheese
- 1 large egg
- 3 tbsp. flour

Directions:

1. Cook the bacon until crispy.
2. Chop the chicken and bacon together in a food processor until fine.
3. Add in the parmesan, egg, flour and mix.
4. Make the patties by hand and fry on a medium heat in a pan with some oil.
5. Once browned, flip over, continue cooking, and lie them to drain.
6. Serve!

Nutrition: Calories: 387 Carbs: 13 g Fat: 16 g Protein: 34 g Fiber: 28 g

16. Cheddar Bacon Burst

Preparation Time: 25 minutes

Cooking Time: 90 minutes

Servings: 8

Ingredients:

- 30 slices bacon
- 2 ½ cups cheddar cheese
- 4-5 cups raw spinach
- 1-2 tbsp. Tones Southwest Chipotle Seasoning
- 2 tsp Mrs. Dash Table Seasoning

Directions:

1. Preheat your fryer to 375°F/190°C.
2. Weave the bacon into 15 vertical pieces & 12 horizontal pieces. Cut the extra 3 in half to fill in the rest, horizontally.
3. Season the bacon.
4. Add the cheese to the bacon.
5. Add the spinach and press down to compress.
6. Tightly roll up the woven bacon.
7. Line a baking sheet with kitchen foil and add plenty of salt to it.

8. Put the bacon on top of a cooling rack and put that on top of your baking sheet.

9. Bake for 60-70 minutes.

10. Let cool for 10-15 minutes before

11. Slice and enjoy!

Nutrition: Calories: 218 Carbs: 20 g Fat: 9 g Protein: 21 g Fiber: 5 g

VEG , LEAN & GREEN AND SALAD RECIPES

17. Baked Portobello, Pasta 'n Cheese

Preparation Time: 10 minutes

Cooking Time: 30 minutes

Servings: 4

Ingredients:

- 1 cup milk
- 1 cup shredded mozzarella cheese
- 1 large clove garlic, minced
- 1 tablespoon vegetable oil
- 1/4 cup margarine
- 1/4 teaspoon dried basil
- 1/4-pound Portobello mushrooms, thinly sliced
- 2 tablespoons all-purpose flour
- 2 tablespoons soy sauce
- 4-ounce penne pasta, cooked according to manufacturer's Directions for Cooking
- 5-ounce frozen chopped spinach, thawed

Directions:

1. Lightly grease baking pan of air fryer with oil. For 2 minutes, heat on 360oF. Add mushrooms and cook for a minute. Transfer to a plate.

2. In same pan, melt margarine for a minute. Stir in basil, garlic, and flour. Cook for 3 minutes. Stir and cook for another 2 minutes. Stir in half of milk slowly while whisking continuously. Cook for another 2 minutes. Mix well. Cook for another 2 minutes. Stir in remaining milk and cook for another 3 minutes.

3. Add cheese and mix well.

4. Stir in soy sauce, spinach, mushrooms, and pasta. Mix well. Top with remaining cheese.

5. Cook for 15 minutes at 390oF until tops are lightly browned.

6. Serve and enjoy.

Nutrition: Calories: 482 Carbs: 32.1g Protein: 16.0g Fat: 32.1g

18. Baked Potato Topped with Cream cheese 'n Olives

Preparation Time: 15 minutes

Cooking Time: 40 minutes

Servings: 1

Ingredients:

- ¼ teaspoon onion powder
- 1 medium russet potato, scrubbed and peeled
- 1 tablespoon chives, chopped
- 1 tablespoon Kalamata olives
- 1 teaspoon olive oil
- 1/8 teaspoon salt
- a dollop of vegan butter
- a dollop of vegan cream cheese

Directions:

1. Place inside the air fryer basket and cook for 40 minutes. Be sure to turn the potatoes once halfway.
2. Place the potatoes in a mixing bowl and pour in olive oil, onion powder, salt, and vegan butter.
3. Preheat the air fryer to 4000F.

4. Serve the potatoes with vegan cream cheese, Kalamata olives, chives, and other vegan toppings that you want.

Nutrition: Calories: 504 Carbohydrates: 68.34g Protein: 9.31g Fat: 21.53g

19. Baked Zucchini Recipe from Mexico

Preparation Time: 10 minutes

Cooking Time: 30 minutes

Servings: 4

Ingredients:

- 1 tablespoon olive oil
- 1-1/2 pounds' zucchini, cubed
- 1/2 cup chopped onion
- 1/2 teaspoon garlic salt
- 1/2 teaspoon paprika
- 1/2 teaspoon dried oregano
- 1/2 teaspoon cayenne pepper, or to taste
- 1/2 cup cooked long-grain rice
- 1/2 cup cooked pinto beans
- 1-1/4 cups salsa
- 3/4 cup shredded Cheddar cheese

Directions:

1. Lightly grease baking pan of air fryer with olive oil. Add onions and zucchini and for 10 minutes, cook on 360oF. Halfway through cooking time, stir.

2. Season with cayenne, oregano, paprika, and garlic salt. Mix well.

3. Stir in salsa, beans, and rice. Cook for 5 minutes.

4. Stir in cheddar cheese and mix well.

5. Cover pan with foil.

6. Cook for 15 minutes at 390oF until bubbly.

7. Serve and enjoy.

Nutrition: Calories: 263 Carbs: 24.6g Protein: 12.5g Fat: 12.7g

20. Banana Pepper Stuffed with Tofu 'n Spices

Preparation Time: 5 minutes

Cooking Time: 10 minutes

Servings: 8

Ingredients:

- ½ teaspoon red chili powder
- ½ teaspoon turmeric powder
- 1 onion, finely chopped
- 1 package firm tofu, crumbled
- 1 teaspoon coriander powder
- 3 tablespoons coconut oil
- 8 banana peppers, top end sliced and seeded
- Salt to taste

Directions:

1. Preheat the air fryer for 5 minutes.
2. In a mixing bowl, combine the tofu, onion, coconut oil, turmeric powder, red chili powder, coriander power, and salt. Mix until well-combined.
3. Scoop the tofu mixture into the hollows of the banana peppers.

4. Place the stuffed peppers in the air fryer.

5. Close and cook for 10 minutes at 3250F.

Nutrition: Calories: 72 Carbohydrates: 4.1g Protein: 1.2g Fat: 5.6g

21. Bell Pepper-Corn Wrapped in Tortilla

Preparation Time: 5 minutes

Cooking Time: 15 minutes

Servings: 4

Ingredients:

- 1 small red bell pepper, chopped
- 1 small yellow onion, diced
- 1 tablespoon water
- 2 cobs grilled corn kernels
- 4 large tortillas
- 4 pieces' commercial vegan nuggets, chopped
- mixed greens for garnish

Directions:

1. Preheat the air fryer to 4000F.
2. In a skillet heated over medium heat, water sauté the vegan nuggets together with the onions, bell peppers, and corn kernels. Set aside.
3. Place filling inside the corn tortillas.
4. Fold the tortillas and place inside the air fryer and cook for 15 minutes until the tortilla wraps are crispy.
5. Serve with mix greens on top.

Nutrition: Calories: 548 Carbohydrates: 43.54g Protein: 46.73g
Fat: 20.76g

22. Black Bean Burger with Garlic-Chipotle

Preparation Time: 10 minutes

Cooking Time: 20 minutes

Servings: 3

Ingredients:

- ½ cup corn kernels
- ½ teaspoon chipotle powder
- ½ teaspoon garlic powder
- ¾ cup salsa
- 1 ¼ teaspoon chili powder
- 1 ½ cup rolled oats
- 1 can black beans, rinsed and drained
- 1 tablespoon soy sauce

Directions:

1. In a mixing bowl, combine all Ingredients and mix using your hands.
2. Form small patties using your hands and set aside.
3. Brush patties with oil if desired.
4. Place the grill pan in the air fryer and place the patties on the grill pan accessory.

5. Close the lid and cook for 20 minutes on each side at 3300F.

Nutrition: Calories: 395 Carbs: 52.2g Protein: 24.3g Fat: 5.8g

SEAFOOD

23. Cajun Spiced Veggie-Shrimp Bake

Preparation Time: 5 minutes

Cooking Time: 20 minutes

Servings: 4

Ingredients:

- 1 Bag of Frozen Mixed Vegetables
- 1 Tbsp. Gluten Free Cajun Seasoning
- Olive Oil Spray
- Season with salt and pepper
- Small Shrimp Peeled & Deveined (Regular Size Bag about 50-80 Small Shrimp)

Directions:

1. Lightly grease baking pan of air fryer with cooking spray. Add all Ingredients and toss well to coat. Season with pepper and salt, generously.
2. For 10 minutes, cook on 330oF. Halfway through cooking time, stir.
3. Cook for 10 minutes at 330oF.

4. Serve and enjoy.

Nutrition: Calories: 78 Carbs: 13.2g Protein: 2.8g Fat: 1.5g

24. Delicious Crab Cakes

Preparation Time: 10 minutes

Cooking Time: 10 minutes

Servings: 4

Ingredients:

- 8 oz. crab meat
- 2 tbsp. butter, melted
- 2 tsp Dijon mustard
- tbsp. mayonnaise
- 1 egg, lightly beaten
- 1/2 tsp old bay seasoning
- 1 green onion, sliced
- 2 tbsp. parsley, chopped
- 1/4 cup almond flour
- 1/4 tsp pepper
- 1/2 tsp salt

Directions:

1. Add all ingredients except butter in a mixing bowl and mix until well combined.
2. Make four equal shapes of patties from mixture and place on parchment lined plate.

3. Place plate in the fridge for 30 minutes.

4. Spray air fryer basket with cooking spray.

5. Brush melted butter on both sides of crab patties.

6. Place crab patties in air fryer basket and cook for 10 minutes at 350 F.

7. Turn patties halfway through.

8. Serve and enjoy.

Nutrition: Calories: 136 Fat,: 12.6 g Carbohydrates: 4.1 g Sugar 0.5 g Protein 10.3 g Cholesterol 88 mg

25. Tuna Patties

Preparation Time: 10 minutes

Cooking Time: 10 minutes

Servings: 2

Ingredients:

- 2 cans tuna
- 1/2 lemon juice
- 1/2 tsp onion powder
- 1 tsp garlic powder
- 1/2 tsp dried dill
- 1 1/2 tbsp. mayonnaise
- 1 1/2 tbsp. almond flour
- 1/4 tsp pepper
- 1/4 tsp salt

Directions:

1. Preheat the air fryer to 400 F.
2. Add all ingredients in a mixing bowl and mix until well combined.
3. Spray air fryer basket with cooking spray.
4. Make four patties from mixture and place in the air fryer basket.

5. Cook patties for 10 minutes at 400 F if you want crispier patties then cook for 3 minutes more.

6. Serve and enjoy.

Nutrition: Calories: 414 Fat,: 20.6 g Carbohydrates: 5.6 g Sugar 1.3 g Protein 48.8 g Cholesterol 58 mg

26. Crispy Fish Sticks

Preparation Time: 10 minutes

Cooking Time: 10 minutes

Servings: 4

Ingredients:

- 1 lb. white fish, cut into pieces
- 3/4 tsp Cajun seasoning
- 1 1/2 cups pork rind, crushed
- 2 tbsp. water
- 2 tbsp. Dijon mustard
- 1/4 cup mayonnaise
- Pepper
- Salt

Directions:

1. Spray air fryer basket with cooking spray.
2. In a small bowl, whisk together mayonnaise, water, and mustard.
3. In a shallow bowl, mix together pork rind, pepper, Cajun seasoning, and salt.
4. Dip fish pieces in mayo mixture and coat with pork rind mixture and place in the air fryer basket.

5. Cook at 400 F for 5 minutes. Turn fish sticks to another side and cook for 5 minutes more.

6. Serve and enjoy.

Nutrition: Calories: 397 Fat,: 36.4 g Carbohydrates: 4 g Sugar 1 g Protein 14.7 g Cholesterol 4 mg

27. Flavorful Parmesan Shrimp

Preparation Time: 10 minutes

Cooking Time: 10 minutes

Servings: 6

Ingredients:

- 2 lbs. cooked shrimp, peeled and deveined
- 2 tbsp. olive oil
- 1/2 tsp onion powder
- 1 tsp basil
- 1/2 tsp oregano
- 2/3 cup parmesan cheese, grated
- 3 garlic cloves, minced
- 1/4 tsp pepper

Directions:

1. In a large mixing bowl, combine together garlic, oil, onion powder, oregano, pepper, and cheese.
2. Add shrimp in a bowl and toss until well coated.
3. Spray air fryer basket with cooking spray.
4. Add shrimp into the air fryer basket and cook at 350 F for 8-10 minutes.
5. Serve and enjoy.

Nutrition: Calories: 233 Fat,: 7.9 g Carbohydrates: 3.2 g Sugar 0.1 g Protein 35.6 g Cholesterol 32 m

SIDES , SAUCE , SOUP AND STEWS

28. Green Beans Rice

Preparation Time: 10 minutes

Cooking Time: 20 minutes

Servings: 4

Ingredients:

- 4 cups water
- 2 cups green beans, trimmed and halved
- 2 cups brown rice
- 4 garlic cloves, minced
- 1 teaspoon nutmeg, ground
- Salt and black pepper to the taste

Directions:

1. In your instant pot, combine the rice with the rest of the ingredients except the green beans, put the lid on and cook on High for 15 minutes

2. Release the pressure fast for 5 minutes, add the green beans, put the lid back on and cook on High for 5 minutes more.

3. Release the pressure fast again for 5 minutes, divide the mix between plates and serve.

Nutrition: Calories: 190 Fat: 6 Fiber 2 Carbs 6 Protein 7

29. Garlic Kale

Preparation Time: 5 minutes

Cooking Time: 5 minutes

Servings: 4

Ingredients:

- 1-pound kale, roughly torn
- ¼ cup chicken stock
- 1 tablespoons spring onion, chopped
- 4 garlic cloves, minced

Directions:

1. In your instant pot, combine all the ingredients, put the lid on and cook on High for 5 minutes.
2. Release the pressure fast for 5 minutes, divide the mix between plates and serve.

Nutrition: Calories: 141 Fat: 5 Fiber 4 Carbs 6 Protein 6

30. Celery and Green Beans Mix

Preparation Time: 10 minutes

Cooking Time: 12 minutes

Servings: 4

Ingredients:

- 1-pound green beans, trimmed and halved
- 1 celery stalk, chopped
- 2 tablespoons olive oil
- 1 red onion, chopped
- 1 cup chicken stock
- 1 tablespoon rosemary, chopped
- Salt and black pepper to the taste

Directions:

1. Set your instant pot on Sauté mode, add the oil, heat it up, add the onion, stir and sauté for 5 minutes.
2. Add the rest of the ingredients, put the lid on and cook on High for 7 minutes
3. Release the pressure fast for 10 minutes, divide between plates and serve.

Nutrition: Calories: 162 Fat: 4 Fiber 3 Carbs 7 Protein 4

31. Parmesan Asparagus

Preparation Time: 5 minutes

Cooking Time: 8 minutes

Servings: 4

Ingredients:

- 3 garlic cloves, minced
- 1 bunch asparagus, trimmed
- 1 cup water
- 3 tablespoons olive oil
- 3 tablespoons parmesan, grated

Directions:

1. Put the water in your instant pot, add the steamer basket, add the asparagus inside, put the lid on and cook on High for 8 minutes.

2. Release the pressure fast for 5 minutes, transfer the asparagus to a bowl, add the rest of the ingredients, toss and serve as a side dish.

Nutrition: Calories: 130 Fat: 4 Fiber 4 Carbs 5 Protein 8

POULTRY AND MEAT

32. Apricot-Glazed Pork Chops

Preparation Time: 15 minutes

Cooking Time: 6 minutes

Servings: 6

Ingredients:

- 6 boneless pork chops
- ½ cup apricot pre**Servings:**
- 1 tablespoon balsamic vinegar
- 2 teaspoons olive oil
- Black pepper to taste

Directions:

1. Add oil to your cooker and heat on "chicken/meat," leaving the lid off.
2. Sprinkle black pepper on the pork chops.
3. Sear chops in the cooker on both sides till golden.
4. Mix balsamic and apricot pre**Servings:** together.
5. Pour over the pork and seal the cooker lid.
6. Adjust cook time to 6 minutes.

7. When time is up, hit "cancel" and quick-release.

8. Test temperature of pork - it should be 145-degrees F.

9. Rest for 5 minutes before serving!

Nutrition: Total Calories: 296 Protein: 20 Carbs: 18 Fat: 16 Fiber: 0

33. Roasted Lamb with Honey

Preparation Time: 5 minutes

Cooking Time: 30 minutes

Servings: 4

Ingredients:

- 1,32 lb lamb
- 2 tablespoons mustard tarragon
- 2 tablespoons rosemary honey
- 2 tablespoons soy
- 1 teaspoon rosemary, chopped
- 2 cloves garlic , minced
- C / N Extra virgin olive
- 0,88 lb potatoes , peeled and chopped
- Salt and black pepper

Directions:

1. Put the meat to macerate the night before with mustard, honey, soy, chopped rosemary, garlic, 1 chorretón oil, salt and pepper.
2. Cook the potatoes and Reserve.
3. Place meat in a preheated Airfryer at 392 ° F for 20 '. Remove and add the potatoes.

4. Return to Airfryer and lower the temperature to 338 ° F

5. When the meat is cooked remove and serve with potatoes.

Nutrition: Calories: 243 Fat: 22g Carbs: 13g Protein: 20g

34. <u>Roasted Lamb with Thyme and Garlic</u>

Preparation Time: 5 minutes

Cooking Time: 30 minutes

Servings: 4

Ingredients:

- 3 pieces of lamb
- 3 cloves of garlic
- olive oil spray
- thyme
- salt pepper

Directions:

1. Season the meat on both sides.
2. Pour a little olive oil spray.
3. Spread crushed garlic on each piece.
4. Preheat airfrer.
5. Put the meat into fryer and add thyme.
6. Wait till meat is fully cooked.
7. Serve.

Nutrition: Calories: 343 Fat: 7g Carbs: 6g Protein: 34g

35. Lamb tagine

Preparation Time: 5 minutes

Cooking Time: 30 minutes

Servings: 4

Ingredients:

- 1,32 lb of shoulder of lamb
- 5,28 oz of white wine
- 0,088 lb of pitted black olives
- 7,04 ml of water
- 0,033 lb fresh ginger
- 0,015 lb of lemon zest
- 1 spoon garlic powder
- 1 spoon oil
- 1 spoon parsley
- 1 spoon of coriander
- 1 dose of saffron
- 1 spoon maizena
- Salt pepper

Directions:

1. Slice the lamb into cubes of 3-4cm and coat the pieces of

   Maizena. Chop the ginger.

2. In a bowl, mix the wine and water.

3. Grate the lemon to obtain 0,015 lb of zest. P

4. Put the olives, ginger, lemon zest, parsley, coriander, saffron and garlic in airfryer - handle side of tank.

5. Arrange the lamb in the bowl opposite the handle. Pour the mixture over the spices. Spread the oil over the lamb. Close the hood.

6. Start cooking.

Nutrition: Calories: 105 Fat: 29g Carbs: 2g Protein: 23g

36. Lamb Fondue

Preparation Time: 5 minutes

Cooking Time: 30 minutes

Servings: 4

Ingredients:

- 1,32 lb of lamb fondue pieces
- 1 eggplant
- 1 zucchini
- 1 red pepper
- 1 liter of cooking oil
- skewers with a diced lamb and eggplant dice
- diced zucchini
- a square of red pepper

Directions:

1. Cut the vegetables into cubes of the same size as the fondue pieces.
2. Fit mini-skewers by varying the vegetables.
3. Cooking is done at the center of the table, with a fondue machine.

Nutrition: Calories: 140 Fat: 0.3g Carbs: 35g Protein: 3g

37. Lamb chops

Preparation Time: 5 minutes

Cooking Time: 30 minutes

Servings: 4

Ingredients:

- Oregano
- Thyme
- Garlic
- Salt
- Pepper

Directions:

1. Preheat your stove with a drizzle of oil.
2. Grab your lamb ribs and place inside. Cook for 4 mins.
3. Your lamb chops should be golden on both sides.

Nutrition: Calories: 279 Fat: 11g Carbs: 13g Protein: 43g

38. Breaded and crispy lamb chops

Preparation Time: 5 minutes

Cooking Time: 30 minutes

Servings: 4

Ingredients:

- 2 eggs
- 8 lean lamb chops
- 0,044 lb of flour
- 0,44 lb breadcrumbs (made of crumbled breadcrumbs)
- 52,79 oz of cooking oil

Directions:

1. Beat the eggs with salt and pepper.
2. Pass the lamb chops first in the flour then in the eggs and finally in the bread crumbs. To obtain a thicker crust, pass the chops again in the eggs and then in the bread crumbs.
3. Heat the oil in the airfryer at approx. 338 ° F.
4. Fry the chops until golden brown.
5. Let them drain on paper towels, sprinkle with salt and pepper to taste and store (uncovered) in an oven at approx.

Nutrition: Calories: 142 Fat: 9.3g Carbs: 5g Protein: 53g

39. Mongolian Beef I

Preparation Time: 5 minutes

Cooking Time: 30 minutes

Servings: 6

Ingredients:

- ¼ cup vegetable stock (you can use vegetable stock cubes or mix. Prepare as per the instructions)
- 2 tablespoons hoisin sauce
- 2 tablespoons oyster sauce
- 1 teaspoon cayenne pepper
- 1½ pound flank steak, thinly sliced
- 2 tablespoons, grapeseed oil
- 3 tablespoons, chopped garlic
- 1 head bok choy, sliced thinly
- 4 green onions cut into 2 inch long slivers
- 2 Asian eggplants, sliced thinly
- 1 tablespoon basil
- 1 tablespoon thyme

Directions:

1. Mix the vegetable stock, hoisin sauce, oyster sauce, and cayenne pepper for the marinade sauce. Dip the beef

slices in the marinade and let is rest in the refrigerator for at least 30 minutes up to one hour. The longer you let the beef marinate, the stronger the flavors are.

2. While the beef is marinating, prepare the vegetables. Turn your stove to medium-high and heat the wok with grapeseed oil. When the oil is hot, add the garlic in first. Allow to brown. Add the vegetables and fry for 5 minutes. Remove from the wok and set aside.

3. Add the beef and the marinade sauce. Cook the beef until browned and the sauce has thickened, which will take up to 5 minutes. Add the vegetables and herbs and mix well. Serve warm.

Nutrition: Calories: 312 Fat: 5g Carbs: 16g Protein: 54g

40. Mongolian Beef II

Preparation Time: 5 minutes

Cooking Time: 30 minutes

Servings: 4

Ingredients:

- 1 pound flank steak, cut into strips
- ¼ cup cornstarch
- 1 teaspoon black pepper
- 1 teaspoon salt
- 1 teaspoon crushed red pepper
- 2 garlic cloves, crushed and minced
- 1 cup soy sauce
- 1 teaspoon sesame oil
- 1 cup brown sugar
- 1 cup water
- 2 cups broccoli florets
- 1 cup carrots, shredded
- 1 cup yellow onion, sliced
- ¼ cup scallions, for garnish if desired

Directions:

1. Mix together the cornstarch, black pepper and salt in a bowl. Take the flank steak strips and toss them in the cornstarch mixture to coat well.

2. Place the steak strips in a large freezer storage bag or other container.

3. To the bag, add the crushed red pepper, garlic, soy sauce, sesame oil, brown sugar, water, broccoli, carrots, and yellow onion.

4. Seal the bag well and shake to mix the ingredients.

5. Serving day: Place contents in a slow cooker. Cook for 6-8 hours on medium to high if frozen, or thaw for 12 hours in the refrigerator, and cook for 4 hours on high.

6. Garnish with scallions, if desired.

Nutrition: Calories: 343 Fat: 23g Carbs: 22g Protein: 14g

OTHERS RECIPES

41. Sunflower Seed Bread

Preparation Time: 15 minutes

Cooking Time: 18 minutes

Servings: 6

Ingredients:

- 2/3 cup whole-wheat flour
- 2/3 cup plain flour
- 1/3 cup sunflower seeds
- ½ sachet instant yeast
- 1 teaspoon salt
- 2/3-1 cup lukewarm water

Directions:

1. In a bowl, mix together the flours, sunflower seeds, yeast, and salt.
2. Slowly, add in the water, stirring continuously until a soft dough ball forms.
3. Now, move the dough onto a lightly floured surface and knead for about 5 minutes using your hands.

4. Make a ball from the dough and place into a bowl.

5. With a plastic wrap, cover the bowl and place at a warm place for about 30 minutes.

6. Grease a cake pan.

7. Coat the top of dough with water and place into the prepared cake pan.

8. Set the cooking time to 18 minutes.

9. Now push the Temp button and rotate the dial to set the temperature at 390 degrees F.

10. Press "Start/Pause" button to start.

11. When the unit beeps to show that it is preheated, open the lid.

12. Arrange the pan in "Air Fry Basket" and insert in the oven.

13. Place the pan onto a wire rack to cool for about 10 minutes.

14. Carefully, invert the bread onto wire rack to cool completely before slicing.

15. Cut the bread into desired-sized slices and serve.

Nutrition: Calories: 132 Total Fat: 1.7 g Saturated Fat: 0.1 g Cholesterol 0 mg Sodium 390 mg Total Carbs 24.4 g Fiber 1.6 g Sugar 0.1 g Protein 4.9 g

42. Date Bread

Preparation Time: 15 minutes

Cooking Time: 22 minutes

Servings: 10

Ingredients:

- 2½ cup dates, pitted and chopped
- ¼ cup butter
- 1 cup hot water
- 1½ cups flour
- ½ cup brown sugar
- 1 teaspoon baking powder
- 1 teaspoon baking soda
- ½ teaspoon salt
- 1 egg

Directions:

1. In a large bowl, add the dates, butter and top with the hot water.
2. Set aside for about 5 minutes.
3. In another bowl, mix together the flour, brown sugar, baking powder, baking soda, and salt.

4. In the same bowl of dates, mix well the flour mixture, and egg.

5. Grease a baking pan.

6. Place the mixture into the prepared pan.

7. Set the cooking time to 22 minutes.

8. Now push the Temp button and rotate the dial to set the temperature at 340 degrees F.

9. Press "Start/Pause" button to start.

10. When the unit beeps to show that it is preheated, open the lid.

11. Arrange the pan in "Air Fry Basket" and insert in the oven.

12. Place the pan onto a wire rack to cool for about 10 minutes.

13. Carefully, invert the bread onto wire rack to cool completely before slicing.

14. Cut the bread into desired-sized slices and serve.

Nutrition: Calories: 269 Total Fat: 5.4 g Saturated Fat: 3.1 g Cholesterol 29 mg Sodium 285 mg Total Carbs 55.1 g Fiber 4.1 g Sugar 35.3 g Protein 3.6 g

43. Date & Walnut Bread

Preparation Time: 15 minutes

Cooking Time: 35 minutes

Servings: 5

Ingredients:

- 1 cup dates, pitted and sliced
- ¾ cup walnuts, chopped
- 1 tablespoon instant coffee powder
- 1 tablespoon hot water
- 1¼ cups plain flour
- ¼ teaspoon salt
- ½ teaspoon baking powder
- ½ teaspoon baking soda
- ½ cup condensed milk
- ½ cup butter, softened
- ½ teaspoon vanilla essence

Directions:

1. In a large bowl, add the dates, butter and top with the hot water.
2. Set aside for about 30 minutes.
3. Drain well and set aside.

4. In a small bowl, add the coffee powder and hot water and mix well.

5. In a large bowl, mix together the flour, baking powder, baking soda and salt.

6. In another large bowl, add the condensed milk and butter and beat until smooth.

7. Add the flour mixture, coffee mixture and vanilla essence and mix until well combined.

8. Fold in dates and ½ cup of walnut.

9. Line a baking pan with a lightly greased parchment paper.

10. Place the mixture into the prepared pan and sprinkle with the remaining walnuts.

11. Set the cooking time to 35 minutes.

12. Now push the Temp button and rotate the dial to set the temperature at 320 degrees F.

13. Press "Start/Pause" button to start.

14. When the unit beeps to show that it is preheated, open the lid.

15. Arrange the pan in "Air Fry Basket" and insert in the oven.

16. Place the pan onto a wire rack to cool for about 10 minutes.

17. Carefully, invert the bread onto wire rack to cool completely before slicing.

18. Cut the bread into desired-sized slices and serve.

Nutrition: Calories: 593 Total Fat: 32.6 g Saturated **Fat:** 14 g Cholesterol 59 mg Sodium 414 mg Total Carbs 69.4 g Fiber 5 g Sugar 39.6 g Protein 11.2 g

SNACKS & APPETIZERS

44. Wrapped Plums

Preparation Time: 5 minutes

Cooking Time: 0 minutes

Servings: 8

Ingredients:

- 2 ounces prosciutto, cut into 16 pieces
- 4 plums, quartered
- 1 tablespoon chives, chopped
- A pinch of red pepper flakes, crushed

Directions:

1. Wrap each plum quarter in a prosciutto slice, arrange them all on a platter, sprinkle the chives and pepper flakes all over and serve.

Nutrition: Calories: 30; Fat: 1 g; Fiber 0 g; Carbs 4 g; Protein 2 g

45. Cucumber Sandwich Bites

Preparation Time: 5 minutes

Cooking Time: 0 minutes

Servings: 12

Ingredients:

- 1 cucumber, sliced
- 8 slices whole wheat bread
- 2 tablespoons cream cheese, soft
- 1 tablespoon chives, chopped
- ¼ cup avocado, peeled, pitted and mashed
- 1 teaspoon mustard
- Salt and black pepper to the taste

Directions:

2. Spread the mashed avocado on each bread slice, also spread the rest of the ingredients except the cucumber slices.

3. Divide the cucumber slices on the bread slices, cut each slice in thirds, arrange on a platter and serve as an appetizer.

Nutrition: Calories: 187; Fat: 12.4 g; Fiber 2.1 g; Carbs 4.5 g; Protein 8.2 g

46. Cucumber Rolls

Preparation Time: 5 minutes

Cooking Time: 0 minutes

Servings: 6

Ingredients:

- 1 big cucumber, sliced lengthwise
- 1 tablespoon parsley, chopped
- 8 ounces canned tuna, drained and mashed
- Salt and black pepper to the taste
- 1 teaspoon lime juice

Directions:

1. Arrange cucumber slices on a working surface, divide the rest of the ingredients, and roll.
2. Arrange all the rolls on a platter and serve as an appetizer.

Nutrition: Calories: 200 Fat: 6 g Fiber 3.4 g Carbs 7.6 g Protein 3.5 g

DESSERTS

47. Vanilla Cake

Preparation Time: 10 minutes

Cooking Time: 25 minutes

Servings: 10

Ingredients:

- 3 cups almond flour
- 3 teaspoons baking powder
- 1 cup olive oil
- 1 and ½ cup almond milk
- 1 and 2/3 cup stevia

- 2 cups water

- 1 tablespoon lime juice

- 2 teaspoons vanilla extract

- Cooking spray

Directions:

1. In a bowl, mix the almond flour with the baking powder, the oil and the rest of the ingredients except the cooking spray and whisk well.

2. Pour the mix into a cake pan greased with the cooking spray, introduce in the oven and bake at 370 degrees F for 25 minutes.

3. Leave the cake to cool down, cut and serve!

Nutrition: Calories: 200 Fat: 7.6 Fiber 2.5 Carbs 5.5 Protein 4.5

48. Pumpkin Cream

Preparation Time: 5 minutes

Cooking Time: 5 minutes

Servings: 2

Ingredients:

- 2 cups canned pumpkin flesh
- 2 tablespoons stevia
- 1 teaspoon vanilla extract
- 2 tablespoons water
- A pinch of pumpkin spice

Directions:

1. In a pan, combine the pumpkin flesh with the other ingredients, simmer for 5 minutes, divide into cups and serve cold.

Nutrition: Calories: 192 Fat: 3.4 Fiber 4.5 Carbs 7.6 Protein 3.5

49. Chia and Berries Smoothie Bowl

Preparation Time: 5 minutes

Cooking Time: 0 minutes

Servings: 2

Ingredients:

- 1 and ½ cup almond milk
- 1 cup blackberries
- ¼ cup strawberries, chopped
- 1 and ½ tablespoons chia seeds
- 1 teaspoon cinnamon powder

Directions:

1. In a blender, combine the blackberries with the strawberries and the rest of the ingredients, pulse well, divide into small bowls and serve cold.

Nutrition: Calories: 182 Fat: 3.4 Fiber 3.4 Carbs 8.4 Protein 3

50. Apple Couscous Pudding

Preparation Time: 10 minutes

Cooking Time: 25 minutes

Servings: 4

Ingredients:

- ½ cup couscous
- 1 and ½ cups milk
- ¼ cup apple, cored and chopped
- 3 tablespoons stevia
- ½ teaspoon rose water
- 1 tablespoon orange zest, grated

Directions:

1. Heat up a pan with the milk over medium heat,
2. add the couscous and the rest of the ingredients, whisk, simmer for 25 minutes, divide into bowls and serve.

Nutrition: Calories: 150 Fat: 4.5 Fiber 5.5 Carbs 7.5 Protein 4